HOW TO SET *Goals* AND REALLY REACH THEM

Mark W. Lee
Simpson College
San Francisco

HOW TO SET
Goals
AND REALLY REACH THEM

MARK LEE

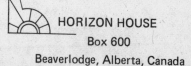

HORIZON HOUSE
Box 600
Beaverlodge, Alberta, Canada

© 1978
Horizon House Publishers
All Rights Reserved
ISBN 0-88965-044-6
HORIZON BOOKS
are published by Horizon House Publishers
Box 600, Beaverlodge, Alberta TOH OCO
Box 16271, Portland, Oregon 97216
Printed in the United States of America

To MARY and PAT ZONDERVAN
mentors, friends, encouragers,
inviting persons to live fully,
happily, biblically
purposefully.

Acknowledgements

For several years my professional work has been made easier to accomplish because of the involvement of my wife, Fern, who provides reading hours and honest critiques; my secretary, Yvonne Cederblom, who types manuscripts repeatedly to serve my constantly changing opinions about what should appear in my writings; and the support of the Simpson College trustees and community, which is beyond my deserts. Without these persons I could not enjoy the privileges of my work. I am indeed grateful.

About the Author

Mark W. Lee has been President of Simpson College, San Francisco, since 1970. Previous to that, he taught at Whitworth College in Spokane, Washington, and at Northwestern College in St. Paul, Minnesota.

While serving at Whitworth, he earned the Ph. D. degree in 1966 from the University of Washington (Rhetoric and Public Address). Previous education includes a diploma from Nyack College, Nyack, New York; B.A. and M.A. degrees from Wheaton College, Wheaton, Illinois; and graduate studies at the University of Minnesota.

Dr. Lee is the author of several books, including his latest two titles: *Our Children: Our Best Friends* and *Creative Christian Marriage*. His lectures are sold in cassette tapes under the LeeSon label and in albums through Promedia, Inc. of California. Articles he has written have appeared in several journals and magazines.

A busy speaker, Dr. Lee has spoken in as many as twenty-seven states and Canada in a single year. For a number of years he spoke to radio audiences on several sustained broadcast series. *Conference Echoes* broadcasts some of his addresses over Family Stations, Inc.

He has served as consultant in communications and management for a number of institutions and industries, including such varied groups as Standard Oil of California, IBM, Credit Union Leagues, the Administrative Management Society, the Veterans Administration, the Civil Service Commission, and a number of State departments, federal agencies, professional organizations and denominations of churches.

Dr. Lee and his wife, Fern, reside in San Francisco. They have four children: Sharon; Mark, Jr.; David and Jody (all adults), and five grandchildren.

Contents

CHAPTER 1

Goals: Gateway to Your Future

Perhaps the most dramatic record of personal purposes and goals available in modern times was published in a story appearing in LIFE Magazine in 1972. At fifteen years of age, John Goddard set down 127 "goals" (actually, they were lifetime purposes) for his future. By age 47 he had achieved 103 of them.

They included: For exploring rivers Goddard selected the Nile, Amazon, Congo, Colorado, Yangtze, Niger, Orinoco and Rio Coco. (In 1972 only the Yangtze, Niger and Orinoco had not been explored.) Goddard also proposed to follow the River Jordan from the Sea of Galilee to the Dead Sea, which remained to be done.

For climbing mountains he selected: Everest, Aconcagua, McKinley, Huascaran, Kilimanjaro, Ararat, Kenya, Cook, Popocatepetl,

Matterhorn, Rainier, Fuji, Vesuvius, Bromo, Grand Tetons, Baldy in California. Ayers Rock in Australia was also listed for climbing. (Only four remained for Goddard to conquer in 1972—Everest, Aconcagua in Argentina, McKinley and Cook in New Zealand.)

For special programs he determined to: carry out a career in Medicine, visit every country in the world, study Navajo and Hopi Indians, learn to fly an airplaine, retrace travels of Marco Polo and Alexander the Great, and ride a horse in the Rose Parade. (This group lacked only the visit to thirty countries to be completed.)

For special projects in photography he chose waterfalls: Iguacu, Victoria, Sutherland, Yosemite, Niagara. (All completed.)

For underwater exploration Goddard recorded: Coral reefs of Florida, Great Barrier Reef off Australia, Red Sea, Fiji Islands, the Bahamas, Okefenokee Swamp and Everglades. (Completed.)

For visiting he specified: North and South Poles, Great Wall of China, Panama and Suez Canals, Easter Island, Galapagos Islands, Vatican City, Taj Mahal, Eiffel Tower, Blue Grotto (Capri), Tower of London, Leaning Tower of Pisa, Sacred Well of Mexico. (Only the Poles, the Great Wall, Easter Island, the

Galapagos remained on the agenda.)

For swimming, the young Goddard proposed to double up some of his other purposes to accomplish two or more on the same adventure by choosing several lakes near the falls he would photograph: Victoria, Superior, Tanganyika, Titicaca, Nicaragua. (Completed.)

For adventure, achievement and cultural development he concluded the list with fifty-five purposes, including: *become* an Eagle Scout, *dive* in a submarine, *land* on and take off an aircraft carrier, *ride* an elephant, camel, ostrich and bronco, *dive* to forty feet, holding breath for two and a half minutes underwater, *catch* a ten-pound lobster and a ten-inch abalone, *play* flute and violin, *type* fifty words a minute, *make* a parachute jump, *learn* water and snow skiing, *go* on a church mission, *study* native medicines and bring back useful ones, *bag* camera trophies of elephant, lion, rhino, cheetah, cape buffalo, and whale, *learn* to fence, *learn* jujitsu, *teach* a college course, *watch* a cremation ceremony in Bali, *explore* the sea depths, *build* his own telescope, *write* a book, *publish* an article in the National Geographic Magazine, *high-jump* five feet, *broad-jump* fifteen feet, *run* a mile in five minutes, *weigh* 175 pounds, *perform* two hundred sit-ups and twenty pull-ups, *learn* French, Spanish and Arabic, *visit* birthplace of Grandfather Sorenson in Denmark, *visit* birthplace of Grandfather Goddard in England, *ship* aboard a freighter as a seaman, *read* the Bible from cover to cover, *read* the works of Shakespeare, Plato, Aristotle, Dickens, Thoreau, Rousseau, Hemingway, Twain, Burroughs, Talmage, Tolstoi, Longfellow, Keats, Poe, Bacon, Whittier and Emerson (not every work of each), *become familiar* with the compositions of Bach, Beethoven, Debussy, Ibert, Mendelssohn, Lalo, Milhaud, Ravel, Rimski-Korsakov, Respighi, Rachmaninoff, Paganini, Stravinsky, Toch, Tschaikovsky, and Verdi, *become proficient* in the use of a plane, motorcycle, tractor, surfboard, rifle, pistol, canoe, microscope, football, basketball, bow and arrow, lariat and boomerang, *play* "Clair de Lune" on the piano, *watch* fire-walking ceremony (in Bali and Surinam), *milk* a poisonous snake, *light* a match with a .22-caliber rifle, *visit* a movie studio, *climb* Cheops' pyramid, *become* a member of the Explorers' Club and the Adventurers' Club, *travel* through the Grand Canyon on foot and by boat, *circumnavigate* the globe (four times), *marry* and have children (has five children). (All of these have been completed.)

Included in this last group, but in 1972 incompleted: *fly* in a blimp, balloon and glider, *own* a horse, chimpanzee, cheetah, ocelot and coyote, *operate* a ham radio, *study* dragon lizards on Komodo Island, *read* the entire Encyclopedia Britannica, *compose* music, *learn* to play polo, *visit* the moon ("someday if God wills"), and *live* to see the twenty-first century.

Thus endeth the dreams, fantasies, hopes, and ambitions of a fifteen-year-old lad. But they did not really end. He recorded them and began a guided life adventure.

By his forty-seventh year he had completed all but two dozen of his life purposes, and many of those remaining were partially completed. In actuality a number were compounded purposes. One or two, like the desire to appear in a Tarzan movie, were, by 1972, dropped by Goddard as childish fantasies, unworthy of adult effort. At the time his story appeared in print, Goddard had just completed his glider ride and his pilot experience. He was in preparation for gaining privilege to enter China to carry through on his purpose to visit the Great Wall.*

As fallout benefit of his lifetime adventure, Goddard became a celebrity, earning as much as $50,000 a year on tour as an adven-

---

LIFE, March 24, 1972, pp. 66-68.

turer-lecturer. When a life quest can become as entrancing as this one by setting purposes and pursuing them, one wonders why the process is not believed and followed by masses of the population.

To help you set and reach goals is the goal of this book.

I can do all things through Christ which strengtheneth me (Philippians 4:13).

CHAPTER 2

Get Ready, Get Set, Aim!

Although every research summary known to me related to goal effectiveness affirms the significant advantage of goal-setting for individuals or institutions, there is not much done by either in setting objectives. And without goals, who can say that an individual or a company has done what should be done to gain efficient use of available resources?

The purpose of this slim volume is to advocate goal-setting for individuals, and institutions as well, although not a great deal will be written about institutions. Goals have been well developed for companies, governments, and churches by students of business. The individual is addressed here even when institutions are cited to illustrate ideas. Group goals are generally effective only if leaders are personal goal-setters. This may account for the number of organizations which state in official guidelines that goal orientation is a primary concern, while investigations show that, in practice, either institutional goals are not well formed, or if formed are seldom carried through as they ought to be.

These chapters are specific. They attempt to meet major issues which repeatedly have been raised in seminars or public meetings where goals have been the central subject. Some features of goal-setting, like time management, have not been accented. They have been adequately treated by other authors. Standard literature related to goals is usually well ordered and should be taken seriously. Some of it, unfortunately, appears so fully oriented for businesses that the individual may lose awareness that goal-setting is primarily for him. Excellent secular materials are available for institutions suggesting time frames, steps, and methods which should be followed to establish goals and see them through to completion. In religious literature the accent remains on the individual.

In these chapters you will discover that goal-setting is hard work. For that reason most persons will not venture, or venturing, will sooner or later abandon effort. Numerous rationalizations arise for not making goals, rationalizations formed commonly to cover laziness. It is to be hoped that laziness, with its insidious cohorts, procrastination and boredom, may be overcome. The rewards are rich for the overcomer.

In examining the sources of personal goals, you will discover some important things about yourself. You may uncover your motivations—why you have done the things you have done, and in that revelation, you will discover why you have not done other things—things you ought to have done. The future awaits you.

Because there is time remaining in life to do many of the things we have always wanted to do, we need to know about processes leading to goals. How do dreams, ambitions, wishes become realities? Can a man or woman, ordinary among peers, make things happen? The answer is yes. Within reason and under God, persons with normal health, intelligence and faith are able to effect significant changes in their lives and, on occasion, in the lives of others.

Practical guides may stimulate verbalization of goals. And goals must be verbalized, stated and studied, reviewed and amended. They are dynamic things, not static. They change, and change back again. Some are dropped, some become larger, and some introduce themselves late in the creative process.

Finally, you will be encouraged to become

a setter of goals for the simple reason that goal-setting works. The things, experiences, family, career, education, spiritual growth that we wish to have and pray for in life are easier to gain through forming meaningful directives for the future than in waiting for accidental results.

At the least, you should be challenged by these few chapters to examine your life, to discover if there may not be some goal, even if it is only one major objective, which will occupy a share of your attention, draw upon your intellect, take a portion of your life in planning and find implementation. The experience of making a thing happen is sufficiently exciting that you will want to do it again, and again.

You will discover that goals are, in my view, not gags, but goads to accomplishment. From earliest times drivers of oxen used pointed sticks to poke the hindquarters of slow or dawdling beasts. The irritation of the jabs made the animals pull harder. The analogy is applied here to persons and goals. Somewhat lazy ourselves and reluctant to perform up to our abilities, we need to manufacture our own goads. We call them goals. Our goals prod us into action.

Some persons believe goals are gags to them and their future freedom. They misunderstand goals, set them clumsily, resist self-discipline or any other stringency. A personal point of view, a philosophy of goal-setting, is vital if the process is going to work. Goal-setting must be affirmed if it is to be effective. Goals must be believed in, understood, acted upon and evaluated.

But now it is up to you. Get ready, get set, aim!

For he looked for a city which hath foundations, whose builder and maker is God (Hebrews 11:10).

CHAPTER THREE

Determine Your Future!

Plans and goals are often equated in this writing. Planning is broader than goal-setting, but cannot be complete without goals. The key word in the process of planning must be "goals." The setting of goals or objectives and the hot pursuit of them may be the most meaningful human cause for success in the experience of persons and institutions. No one can know how much failure in private life and public affairs may be attributed to a lack of planning and goal-setting.

GOALS AND PURPOSES

Goals should be differentiated from purposes, not merely because there is a difference, but because through this refinement goals may be sharply defined, nudging participants into more effective ways of setting them. A goal is measurable, whereas a purpose is not. Anyone given the privilege of doing so may check results and conclude that I have succeeded or failed in achieving a goal. Purposes are too broad for practical measurement.

Goals are specific: purposes are general.

If on New Year's Day I inform my family that I will be a better father and husband next year, I have announced a purpose. In this general sense, measurement of my improvement as a husband is not inherently verifiable. One child believes I improved; a second may not perceive improvement. He may feel there has been decline.

On the other hand, if I announce that I am going to save $500 during the next calendar year, I have announced a goal. Any person examining my bank books discovers whether I succeeded or failed. I will know, and others may know, if I permit them to check, whether my goal, a specific thing, has been achieved. Why? Because I had stated a time frame in which it was to happen. A time frame is the clearest factor in measuring success or failure in goals.

The words "goal" and "purpose" are often used as synonyms because *measurement* of success or failure is not commonly understood as vital to goals and unknown for purposes. This oversight on specificity may be illustrated in a news item reported in a leading magazine:

> A survey by the Institute of Life Insurance shows that 80 percent of Americans over 18 chose "a happy family life" as their Number One goal. Only 3 percent chose "making a lot of money" and 4 percent voted for "a fulfilling career."*

None of the three items in the paragraph reference is a goal. No one knows specifically what a "happy family" is, although it is an appropriate and important purpose to set. My family is happy in a Christian role assignment for each member. Other families, mostly secular, tell me they cannot be happy in that context. No one knows what a "lot of money" is. A million dollars is about right for one, and two thousand dollars comprise a treasure for another. "A fulfilling career" for one person is a bore for a second.

A person's value system and interests are involved in the experiences he chooses for his life. Everyone has general feelings about what he believes, and even random decisions are partly guided by the values each cherishes. But the value system is made specific through individual goal-setting. All references in the

---

Christianity Today, Aug. 20, 1974, p. 44.

above quotation are purposes which, for each individual, may most likely be achieved through setting and accomplishing goals. Without goals those "Americans" may expect to miss many of their hopes and expectations for family and career.

SUCCESS AND GOAL ORIENTATION

Anyone who seriously wishes to succeed in his personal life and profession should adopt goal orientation as a primary concern. Why? No human method to success is held in higher regard among analysts than determining goals and energetically applying them.

Unfortunately, men and women devoted to the Scriptures may resist goal-setting on the rationalization that the Bible seems to stress the value of a current day, this day in which one finds himself. Usually they use one translation and fail to make comparisons to discover the actual meaning of the passages cited. The most commonly quoted verses are Matthew 6:25 and James 4:13-15.

The Matthew passage, however, concludes that persons of faith should not worry about tomorrow. Clearly, worry is the writer's issue, not goal-setting. If anything, the setting of goals will prevent or reduce worry.

The James passage does not discourage

goal-setting, but goal-setting without God's participation. The passage warns against pride and egotism. The reader of James is commanded to plan in God's will. Careful analysis of these and similar passages corroborates the idea of goal-setting, of projecting oneself into the future in an appropriate way, with personal humility and trust in God.

Specific biblical passages relate to goals. For example, Abram's father, Terah, accepted the goal to make Canaan his residence and moved from Ur of the Chaldees to complete his pledge. Arriving at Haran, the goal was dropped. Terah's interest flagged. After Terah died, Abram completed the goal with his nephew, Lot (Genesis 11:31-12:5).

It is easy to list purposes and goals of characters who make up the biblical narratives. Job maintained spiritual goals to benefit his children. David made both long-range goals and short-range goals. His men on one occasion determined to get water from Bethlehem's well (an immediate goal) to please their leader. One of David's eminent goals was to build a temple. God rejected the goal, but permitted Solomon to pick it up and implement it. The returning remnant, centuries after Solomon's reign, appeared to emulate Solomon by setting construction goals to restore Jerusalem's wall and temple.

The Apostle Paul was an effective goal-setter, mapping out massive missionary projects, determining to have Timothy come to him "before winter" (II Timothy 4:21); to spend the "winter" with the Corinthians (I Corinthians 16:6); and to spend another "winter" in Nicopolis (Titus 3:12). Other personal references reveal his goal orientation.

The apostle's normal activity and life direction illustrate well how goal-oriented persons live their lives. He followed personal prescriptive patterns of conduct from day to day, season to season, in order to carry out the long-range goals of life. On the occasion of Paul's journey to Rome, a specific goal, his friends tried to dissuade him from going toward the intermediate goal, the trip to Jerusalem. But Paul remained adamant about his decision (Acts 21:13-14). Jesus Himself followed the pattern of goal-setting, sometimes with eminent firmness, as when He "set his face to go to Jerusalem" (Luke 9:51).

TIME IS FUTURE

Sometimes goal-setting is resisted because of a misperception of time. All the time that you and I have left in life is the future. Even the present is so fleeting that it barely deserves mention. In fact, it is but a fractional moment that separates past from future. All that has preceded (the past) this moment (the present) is completed. Whether memory of the past takes me back to a minute ago when this paragraph was begun, or to my childhood of decades ago makes no difference—the past is history. Whether an event occurred two minutes ago, two days ago, two years ago, two decades ago, or two millennia ago—it is history. I may learn from it and live through the consequences of it, but it is completed. My hope for life meaning is entirely futuristic, and I live wisely in this fleeting, present, fractional moment when I use it to guide my future. The future, both near and far, makes the present meaningful.

Since this concept of time applies to each life, a person should feel virtually compelled to formulate goals. But this means he intends to influence meaningfully that future, the only one he has. Why should it be lived by accident, even granting that most general accidents of life are somewhat beneficial? A man finds a job. Could he, by goal-setting, find a better one or one more to his liking? He moves to a community. Could he, by goal-setting, choose another better suited to his interests? It is likely that he can, and he should.

There is a perceptive insight which only a few persons seem to know about and follow—"bringing the future up to the present." It affirms that if I am clear about what I want to do in my future, and maintain efficiency with my current obligations, I am free to live my future. If I write a letter today which I would ordinarily write tomorrow, I have brought tomorrow up to the present.

As I write these sentences I am enjoying a modest euphoria. It is April. My writing goals included a title for last year (done and published), and one for this year (complete and scheduled for release in November). This title was planned for next year. My writing goals are thirteen months ahead of schedule. By that schedule advancement my future has been brought into my present. It feels good—very good indeed.

One writer summarized the challenge of goal-setting, bringing the future into the present: "Wise people make their own future. They give themselves heart and soul to something beyond the satisfaction of today's wants. They do not give credence to fate and destiny and waves of the future. Those are abstract things. Instead, they consider the ways in which to determine their own future right now."*

Determining your future now—that is the challenge of setting goals.

---

*The Royal Bank of Canada Monthly Letter, November 1974, p. 2.

We can make our plans, but the final out-come is in God's hands. . . . We should make plans—counting on God to direct us (Proverbs 16:1, 9, LB).

CHAPTER FOUR

Objections Overruled!

Despite goal-setting's apparent advantages, many people still resist the idea. For what reasons?

1. *Because it seems to violate faith principles.* I have previously alluded to this in reference to biblical passages (usually from older and somewhat archaic translations) which are not well exegeted or understood by most laymen (e.g., Matthew 6:25; James 4:13-15).

It is my view that goal-setting persons are men and women of greater faith than those who do not set goals. Their faith for the future urges them forward to exploits. Because human imagination is vivid and creates unrealistic expectations or hopes, each person must carefully track his life in order to get the most out of it. If we are impractical we may either expect too much or too little.

Our friends, even we ourselves, provide illustrations of unrealized hopes. They may be generalized. The man of excess has a score or more major projects in mind. He makes false starts on many. Seldom will one be completed. He is easily frustrated, drops half-finished programs, and seems to become a victim of his own stalled puberty when energy was high, direction low and tolerances limited.

Or he may be a man of the majority, basically lazy and living life "as it comes, one day at a time." Because he does not set goals he does not perceive much value in what he is doing at any precise moment. He is often bored. This is understandable when, as T. S. Eliot stated, our lives are measured out with "coffee spoons." Each day seems an inconsequential bit of life, a coffee spoonful of life, but the wise man knows that his life is the sum total of his days. The Grand Canyon could be dug with a coffee spoon if the digger were patient and lived long enough. A full life is a life of full days.

Being lazy, a person appears prepared to accept boredom in the place of excitement, because, although he prefers an exciting life, too much effort is required to gain it. To live with this human frailty, if he is a Christian, he sometimes rationalizes that goal-setting is unbiblical, unspiritual and presumptuous. Goal-setting means "running ahead" of God, or even "playing God." This religiosity makes neglect, laziness and ignorance appear to be genuine spirituality. Planning, hard work, focus and faith for a future are distorted and alleged to be pagan or carnal. In fact, they are important to genuine Christian success.

2. *Because it often produces guilt feelings.* What will happen to my reputation with God if I set a goal and miss it? What will happen to my self-esteem? The answers to these questions are that one's reputation is not in danger with God unless he attempts nothing at all. And self-esteem may be greatly strengthened by realistic goals. If one does not set a few more goals than he can make, he is likely not setting enough goals.

As long as persons confuse morals and goals they will feel guilty when they do not complete their goals. Moral laws are to be kept without violation. When they are broken, the violator should confess his failure and improve his conduct. Moral laws relate to the nature of man, his spiritual and personal integrity, and what God prefers for man's conduct and good. Goals are different. They are means to ends, presumably laudatory purposes. They are ways in which an individual or institution commits the future, or wishes to commit it.

Because the future is unknown to mortals

there is no assurance that a goal can be achieved. Promises will be broken, someone will die, a job will be terminated, the economy will change, new factors will be introduced, and other amendments will be voluntarily introduced by the goal-setter. Goals will have to be changed, exchanged, dropped, added. Some are important, some are not. Some are weak, some are strong. They are dreams, not morals. They remain only dreams unless processes are inaugurated and commitments are made for their achievement. Through goals dreams become realities. If goals are not achieved, they are not to be repented of, even though the person setting them may expect to feel deep disappointment.

The issues related to goal-setting are not moral, although goals related to morals may be formulated. Such goals relate to the moral and ethical conduct of individuals, but even for these the goal-setting process is largely neutral. That process should not be avoided for fear of failure.

Goals may be likened to automobiles, which are neither good nor evil. The driver may use a vehicle for good or for ill. Whether the car is driven in a safe or dangerous manner is determined by him. In the same way, goals may be either good or evil.

The Nazi designs of the 1930's serve to illustrate goals that were evil. One ambitious aim was to eliminate all influences felt to "dilute Aryan purity." Another was simply to control the people (this was based on the premise that the state was supreme and could override individual rights). Pursuing these goals, the Nazis proceeded to sterilize the color-blind (to prevent the problem from spreading) and even attempted to eradicate the Jewish race.

But this does not denigrate goal-setting. Goal orientation was not, and is not, evil because it may be used by evil men.

If a goal is unethical (reason for a sense of guilt) the person is at fault as a person, not because of goals or because of goal-setting. Objectives in the life of an energetic, ethical, serving individual make him more effective in gaining his purposes and doing things needed by society. In the life of an evil, self-serving person goals will assist in achieving selfish, antisocial behavior. When morals are at stake, one's concern should not be with goals, but with the individual who is in an ethical skirmish.

Opposition to goals may generally be viewed as distortion of goal orientation. This may be illustrated in the objections of Charles

McCabe, an eminent San Francisco columnist. In his column he praised a man for having no goals, asserting that he had himself labored under the burden of his own goals. This brought him almost to a nervous breakdown. He wrote: "Goals are terrible prisons."

Purging himself of goals, McCabe believed his life improved in quality. Without goals, he believed that at age forty-four he stumbled into the writing of a column. "It didn't take me long," stated McCabe, "to realize that I wanted to write a column more than anything in life. I had achieved a goal without knowing I had one."*

What a loss, to wait unnecessarily to age forty-four, a loss a competent goal-setter would not permit to happen. To cast for his goals (again, not to be confused with morals as he did) McCabe might have discovered fifteen or twenty years earlier that he wished to be a columnist, that he could prepare himself for that career and participate longer in it. Genuine understanding of goals by any person would never permit him to relate goals to a prison. They are fun. They are guidelines to entrancing games of serious living.

The writer, McCabe, having criticized

San Francisco Chronicle, February 2, 1978.

goals, believing them to be gags rather than goals, actually discovered a purpose in his life and began to cultivate it. Once a purpose was discovered by him, it became liberating, almost life-giving. If such a discovery of one's talents and potential may be found in the awareness of purpose, motivation follows. Our purpose here is to make the discovery as soon as possible in the course of life.

To miss a goal is to miss a point or two in a game. One reason why games like football, baseball and other sports are so popular is that they are clearly goal-oriented. The goals are simple and possible to achieve during a short time period of play—an hour or two. The goal is to carry the ball a hundred yards, or to hit it in a way that permits a runner to take base. All goals are to be achieved according to the rules of the game. The inner feelings of players and spectators relate to justice, and when there is a violation of justice there follows altercation between players, referees, and even fans.

The lesson is clear—a game is goal-oriented and should be played by the rules. When it is, life is fun, things get done, and the worth of persons appears more clearly. Life is fair play when played by the rules.

3. *Because it requires careful analysis.*

Men and women know something about cause and effect, but they tend to leave it to the scholars to find causes and effects. The general population discovers that thinking through matters and solving difficult problems are too much trouble. Treating symptoms is easier than digging for sources. Palliatives are simpler than cures. Band-Aids are sometimes applied to problems requiring major surgery.

Events are, as we have said, accidents of life. Much of what happens is our reaction to what is available. Families live from paycheck to paycheck. As a consequence, bills are paid as pressures mount and no plan is designed and followed for the dispersal of family funds. Children go to school without adequate goals for use of their education. (No wonder they are bored.) Church is to be reacted to, not a place for one's own participation and constructive activity. A job is for moneymaking, not for the future with its personal service and development. The good reasons for conduct are missing. The business of living cannot, under these circumstances, be anything but unhappy and unsatisfactory.

Goals make the human difference. An incident in the life of our younger daughter illustrates that difference. Jody attended a high school nationally known for its academic orientation. Students could take some courses generally available only to collegians. One of these was human anatomy and Jody registered for it.

During the first half of the course she was bored, did only a little better than passing work, and complained about what she had to do. Almost overnight her attitude changed. She expressed her excitement in the course, her grade elevated, and she began to share with us some of the material she was learning.

When we asked about the reasons for the turnaround in her attitudes and motivation, she answered immediately, "When I decided that I might become a missionary, I realized that I might be doing some nursing. If I did, anatomy would be important. I felt like I had a good reason to diligently study this subject."

Who can doubt that clear purposes and goals would improve motivations for most students as they did for Jody? They certainly changed my own life for good from late high school through completion of a doctoral program at a university.

Anyone who has worked with college students for a time knows how very different they are in evaluating their schools. Most have a love/hate feeling about their institutions. But is is rather easy to discover those who are happiest, most satisfied, and moving with enthusiasm toward commencement. They are the ones who have goals. They perceive their college to be a means to a good end for them.

This is observed most clearly among the married students. They live in cramped quarters on the edge of the campus, or in some poverty-stricken area of town. Their mates are animated, care for babies, and maintain a fairly even household.

What makes this possible? Goals! The large goal is to complete college, at least get one member through. There is little time for complaint about lack of time, lack of money, or anything else. The goal is everything, and it stimulates the best character in the members of the young family.

To set realistic and meaningful goals, a person must be honest with himself and with family members—and they with him. He must acknowledge his strengths and weaknesses, the advantages he has working for him and those that have been left out. He, and those whose lives are woven into his, must evaluate where they find themselves, where they wish to go in five or ten years or more, and how they may arrive there.

This means they may have to evaluate their life-style (it may have to be altered), they may have to evaluate the education of one or more members (someone may have to go back to school), or they may need an expert opinion (not enough is known about some matters). This list of preparatory activities could be extended, depending upon the purposes at issue.

Goal-setting for persons who, for a number of years, have conducted their lives by accidents—just letting things happen—can be disruptive, even traumatic. Certainly, it becomes hard work, if for no other reason than that it has never been done by these persons before. But there are other reasons, like the dynamic process which places goals in a flexible context, ever changing and shifting to meet new insights and conditions. Goal-setting is a strange and fearful thing for those who have not engaged in it. And it is more difficult to start the process as a person gets older.

Most people give up. To set goals is difficult enough, but they must be monitored to assure their achievement. The process is dynamic, fluctuating, changing, but basic. If at first a simple goal or two may be set by a person and followed through, a sense of victory, even euphoria, may stimulate larger efforts. A private goal to improve some aspect of one's personal life, a renovation project for the home or property, or a shift in a job assignment might start the process.

One thing the goal-setter learns: once the process is begun and the sweet taste of success is experienced, nothing else can quite take the place of this way of life. He feels like an evangelist who would convert the world, if he could, to the goal-directed life under God. He knows that goals are the manifestation of God's gift to thinking and energetic persons—the dignity of choice.

The soul of the sluggard desireth, and hath nothing: but the soul of the diligent shall be made fat (Proverbs 13:4).

CHAPTER FIVE

Where Do Goals Come From?

For most persons common "goals," if they appear at all, arise out of the course of live events. They may or may not be satisfactory. They may not have been selected and evaluated by persons affected by them. They are accidents, as we have said, which occur as men and women move along in life carried by the streams of events. "Accidents," as the word is used in this writing, does not imply tragedy. It is used to compare the unplanned (accidental) life to the planned (purposeful).

A life of pleasant accidents is sufficiently gratifying to many men and women. They may never think about the life they could have created by designing their futures.

I may meet a friend accidentally as I walk down the street. I report to my wife at dinner that in the course of another activity I "accidentally" encountered our friend. The exchange of conversation with my friend was short and pleasant. Both of us wished that we could have extended our visit. Had we planned properly (made an appointment), we could have had lunch together, could have extended the conversation, could have enjoyed ourselves more.

It is possible that a coincidence will be beneficial in that a person is "discovered" by press agents and made a celebrity, or by accident of birth he falls into a generous inheritance. But for every happy chance event there are myriads of uneven experiences, and some catastrophic losses. For each windfall there are thousands who experience no meaningful benefit. Low odds suggest that it is folly to leave success to chance. Especially is the error tragic when goal-setting can effectively improve the quality of life for a majority of human beings.

INADEQUATE SOURCES

Goals may be set by *friends*. A common tragedy among youths is to follow the immediate shallow objectives set for them by their peers. Accelerating to a hundred miles an hour, smoking a "joint," taking a drink, quitting a class, living together without marriage, and a thousand other simplistic and immediate actions are proposed. They are "quickie" goals, requiring no thought or planning. Some are followed because of peer pressure or style popularity and because there seems to be no better goal available at the moment.

We do not know how many aims of one person are foisted upon another just to gain fellowship or personal control of another's life. Persons may exploit others for their own reinforcement. A man may flag in his own resolve unless another is enlisted on his side. He is at least temporarily incapable of thinking and acting for himself. He may wish to be accepted by the group. The herd instinct grows and distracts him.

The problems related to being youthful may prevent the setting of large and important goals by children or even collegians. Elders have permitted distractions to interfere and rob children of meaningful guidelines for their lives. Many youthful goals either fail or are unsatisfactory in that they are not related to long-range goals or constructive purposes. Einstein once observed, "Perfection of *means* and confusion of *goals* characterize our age."

A young person planning nearly ten years ahead of his present situation is almost assured success. Even if he is not as successful as he hoped, he gains more, because of planning, than he would have gained had he not set objectives.

Goals may be set by *circumstances*. Persons are often guided by situations rather than guiding them. Physical infirmities, poverty, accidents, disappointments and the like are permitted to immobilize or confuse overly submissive men and women. It is acknowledged that some events, like nationwide depression or warfare, carry great force, but it is also true that many men and women, by realistic goal-setting, blunt the force of painful situations. What are otherwise debilitating circumstances may be turned for benefit by enterprising managers.

Individual goals for a person may be set by his *family*. Certainly family aims should be set by family members. But our concern is with goals for individuals—one person at a time. Parents generally believe they know what is best for their children and may attempt to force their values upon those children long after independence should have been given to, or taken by, the children.

A gentleman of my acquaintance retained a job he hated because of the persuasive approach of his parents whose intentions of security and income were substituted for his goals of early-life adventure in work, study and travel. He would have, in time, become a family man and hard worker, but he was not able to break away from the domination of his parents who, unwittingly, condemned him to a life of drudgery.

Certainly, parental interests ought to play a part in assisting children to set objectives for themselves, but goals should be based upon much more than the wishes and wisdom of mother and father. Parents should seek to help their children discover their potential abilities and talents. These imply the objectives to be set by that individual.

Goals may be set by generation *styles*. From decade to decade there are favorite pastimes and professions which appear attractive to young men and women. A leading style or influence in one's generation may weight the matter too heavily.

The idea is readily illustrated. Among Christian young men and women during a decade or so following student uprisings in the mid-1960s there arose an antichurch attitude. Extra- or para-church groups of Christians formed home meetings and were sometimes polarized by their common resistance to the institutional church and an ordained clergy.

During this period fewer youth applied for denominational church service, although many young Christians confessed interest in missionary effort and acknowledged the imperative of the Great Commission of Jesus to preach the gospel to all peoples. When challenged with the opportunities, Christian students were caught in a dilemma of contending for basic Christianity but experiencing relatively meager spiritual growth. They were also hard put to discover new places to advance the Christian cause. What they did was done with little hope their efforts would survive them.

The antichurch fad robbed many zealous youths of the option to serve great needs in places of the world where only the institutional church was ministering, and only the church would be permitted to minister. (Many of those independents later entered the institutional church which a few years before they criticized. Some turned toward totalitarian or authoritative sectarian "churches.")

Goals may be set by casual *experiences*, especially those in college or even high school. Many students are distracted by the popular movements in the schools they attend.

A well-known entertainer and writer began his career as a teacher. He taught Spanish. When asked why he became a teacher, and why Spanish, he said that one of the finest instructors he ever encountered in his student days was a Spanish teacher. That teacher motivated him and others by his ability as a teacher and his love for Spanish.

Pliable youths were made into Spanish teachers because the style of the school was set, in part, by this animated language professor. It took a few years before several of the budding Spanish tutors discovered they should have made occupational decisions on other criteria than love for their teacher.

For several years in a college which I attended there were more than ordinary numbers of students who felt destined to become cultural anthropologists. I was one of them. The head of the department was excessively popular. His students persuaded other students to become anthropology majors. In most instances the students were not projected into graduate studies to which their favorite professor was prepared to commit them. And then he was gone. Many of us were destitute and unwilling to accept someone else as our teacher and mentor. My own shift in emphasis turned out to be advantageous for me, a shift for which I was better suited then my first commitment.

During the years of student demonstrations following 1964 there were many students lost to colleges and universities who dropped out of formal education because of the wind shifts in youthful interests and attitudes. During ensuing years counselors in the field rediscovered returning former students who had terminated their collegiate programs for what they believed to be the movement of the future. They had been caught up in the emotional pitch which characterized the period. When the cacophony of voices subsided, many requested the privilege of returning to school and picking up their programs.

Others felt they had sacrificed too much time. They could not coax themselves to another start. Many were disillusioned. Some dropped out of the mainstream of society. Perhaps the knotty problems could have been solved or avoided or moderated if the students had set goals and found means for achieving them.

I am convinced there would have been a difference. Anyone informed about the research on the benefits of formal education will likely doubt that the student should drop his formal education. As a general rule, it is well to complete a college program. The criticisms and fault-finding in this matter generally come from persons who had no idea why they were in school or what to study while they were there. The failure in setting objectives is unrecognized, but the failure is felt, and the college is blamed for the feeling.

SELF SOURCES

Goals ought to emerge from oneself, from the mind, if not the soul. Something inside a person ought to inspire a meaningful response to the call of the future. There should be a belief, within reasonable dimensions, in the potential of a human being. He can do almost anything (again, within reason) he wishes to do.

Why, then, do most of the millions of human beings on earth go through life on their hands and knees? Because they are unaware of the degree to which they control their lives, their minutes and days, which can be directed toward meaningful experiences, adventure and service.

Could not much of the tension in society, especially the tension between generations, be relieved, at least to a meaningful degree, by encouraging youths to set purposes/goals and follow them? Consider the achievements of John Goddard, who at age fifteen set down the goals outlined in chapter one. Surely parents assisting their children to achieve worthy goals would not devote more time and money to those projects than they do in their present attempts to repair broken relationships and shore up the damage created by unguided lives casting about for something to do.

Each person should sense his obligation to plan his life. Other human beings seem bent upon planning much of my life, so why should not I have something significant to say about it? Parents condition children, teachers bend the twigs, advertisers persuade us to buy products, and the like. The only way I can gain control of my affairs is to pick and choose or reject various proposals and options for my future. Under God, I become the captain of my "fate." Or to cast the idea and challenge in better terms, I must "work out my salvation with fear and trembling" (Philippians 2:12).

Each person should have faith that a controlled or guided life is better than one driven by accidents and chance experiences. Many devoted men and women assume that faith "waits," and presumption "acts." My own belief is that faith "acts." Presumption is acting without faith—without faith that God is at work to check, monitor, assist, delay, even stop the actions of those who trust Him.

"Waiting" is often an excuse for inaction, and may assume elements of magic in it. The biblical injunction to "wait" upon the Lord is a concept of prayer and devotion, not to be invoked against planning.

Faith is action at its best. As I perceive it, God is able, even willing, to *close* doors in my life. I proceed, not presumptuously but with the best insight available to me, to do what I feel ought to be done. All is to be touched by prayer. I am stopped or turned, and earnestly wish to be, when I am overextending. My friend believes that he should wait "until doors *open*" before he is willing to move. He believes God *opens* doors, but does not believe He *closes* them, except later when events do not go well for him.

There should be a commitment to the belief that one can make things happen. Goethe wrote: "What you can do, or dream you can, begin it: Boldness has genius, power and magic in it." (I reject the idea of "magic," but Goethe used the word as descriptive rather than actual in meaning.)

Assuming that an individual is without severe physical or mental handicaps, he may expect that he will be able to do just about anything he wishes to do, or to come sufficiently close that he and those nearest to him will be gratified with the results.

Full achievement of a goal is not mandatory for satisfaction. Robert Taft set out to become President of the United States, as his father was before him. He missed, but on the way became a senator from Ohio, and was voted by his colleagues as one of the five greatest senators to serve in Congress. The other four named were La Follette, Clay, Calhoun and Webster.

Illustrations could be multiplied from biographies of successful persons who, through purpose and goal-setting, became eminent. They often expressed their own surprise at their success, and generally attributed their achievements to planning and projecting their futures.

As a young man, Robert S. Kerr of Oklahoma determined to be married, become a millionaire, and be elected the governor of Oklahoma—in that order. He achieved them all, and also became a United States senator from his state. Briefly, in 1960 he was touted to become a candidate for the nomination of his party to the presidency of the United States.

A dramatic personal experience also bears out this claim—that one can make an event happen. Our son, David, moved to San Francisco with his wife and their infant daughter. Husband, wife and child, renting temporary quarters, wished to have their own home. My wife and I agreed and encouraged them to find a house to buy. Their resources were low, but we were prepared to advance our limited funds to them.

One Saturday, before noon, David and Suzanne came to our home. They were discouraged about the problem, more deeply than I had ever seen them. In the development of the conversation, our son said, "Make us understand how to make your goals system work for us."

"I believe it is a practical system. It will work," I said.

"Okay. Make it work for us."

"You mean that you wish for me to buy your house for you?" I asked.

"Yes, I don't think I wish to look any more," David replied.

"Well, I can find the house, but I feel funny about doing so. I wouldn't want someone to choose my house for me."

"I doubt that anyone can find a home around here for the money we can pay."

His statement was like waving a red flag

before me. I had to look for a house. I turned to our daughter-in-law. "Come on," I said, "we will find a house."

Suzanne was excited and ready to go in a few moments.

"When should I have dinner ready?" my wife laughingly asked.

"Same time as always. We will be home in time for dinner."

Suzanne and I left amid the encouraging remarks, glad-handing, and friendly skepticism of David.

"We will not return," I said, "until we have a house. But we will be home in time for dinner."

Suzanne and I drove the neighborhood, talked to several realtors, looked at several addresses which she had seen before but had done nothing about. Within four hours we found the house, negotiated a price based on the cash we could raise, and purchased the property. We arrived home more than two hours before dinner and took everyone over to see the acquisition. It was a happy moment.

David smiled his broad smile, and said, "I'll never doubt your goal-setting again. I have seen it before and should never have doubted it."

Several years later, when Suzanne and

David moved to a distant city to complete his graduate education, they sold their home at a handsome profit, enough to launch themselves well in the new city. In a matter of a few days they had a home selected and purchased in the new location.

They learned the lesson—making things happen. They continue to do so.

... work out your own salvation with fear and trembling. For it is God which worketh in you both to will and to do of his good pleasure (Philippians 2:12-13).

CHAPTER SIX

Setting Goals—The Wrong Way

Goals may be wrongly set by following wrong processes. Here is how it happens:

BELIEVING FALSE INFORMATION

It is well known that persons may receive false information about anything, including themselves. Wrong, inadequate or otherwise unsatisfactory information is imposed or communicated, and if we act on it we shall be disappointed with the outcomes of our decisions. When we do act in this way we tend to blame something other than ourselves. The goal-setting process itself may be blamed. The fault is not in the legitimate process but in clumsy treatment of goal orientation.

One form of misinformation is wrong or incomplete self-evaluation. We may believe ourselves to be talented in ways we are not.

My wife and I were engaged in a couples' conference at a well-known Christian center in California. The fee for the program was higher-than-average. Everything but one matter about the conference seemed to be carefully planned and appointed. The young man engaged to provide both the musical direction for the group and the solo work was inept. He had no training in music, and revealed no aptitude in the field. He could not chord well his guitar, and whatever key he chose for the instrument was not the one he sang. The words were sometimes jumbled, sometimes forgotten. These lapses were followed by fumbling for something to say or do.

Many members of the group were embarrassed for him. It turned out that he had been engaged because a couple in the group had recommended him on the basis of his sincerity as a Christian young man. The couple had not heard him before this time. His friends discovered that their confidence was not justified as that confidence related to musical talents.

However, no one doubted the sincerity of the young man, or his desire to develop as a spiritual leader. The group was gracious, permitting the youth to complete his weekend assignment. In a form of benediction, before the conference broke up, all attendees were requested to take hands, forming a great circle, and opportunity was given for any participants to pray aloud. The young man began to pray—thanking God for his talent, for his opportunity to share his music with the group, for the encouragement he felt to give his life for this particular ministry, and for the privilege of helping others to share music which honors the best that God gives to His children.

The fellow, although a sincere and devoted Christian, was not a musician, and would not likely ever become one. He was wrong about his abilities and talents. Someone in the field of music needed to talk with him. This could only be ideally done if he should seek the opinions of those he respected in music styles related to his interests. He could always strum a guitar and sing for his own self-expression, but there was no future public ministry of music for him. He was totally unaware of the perception others had of his efforts. He relied on his private opinion of himself, and projected that as God's perception. He had false information.

NEGLECTING PROCESSES

Persons commonly fail simply by neglecting the processes for discovering objectives.

They believe that God will guide their futures without human participation. They feel that God's will is irresistible for persons of integrity and devotion. For them Christian faith is made somewhat magical. By this magic God's will is imposed upon daily life events. The accidents of life are presumed to be acts of God to which pious persons acquiesce. Perhaps this is the most common belief about life's experiences held by evangelical Christians.

The idea of living by life's daily accidents never seemed more unsatisfactory to me than it did one day in May, 1975, in Cleveland, Ohio. Mr. Donald Seibert, Chief Executive Officer and Chairman of the Board of the J. C. Penney Company, spoke to a breakfast meeting of Christian men, nearly 1,000 in number, on the subject of goal-setting. He argued both from the biblical and secular evidence that goal orientation was an important factor in success for the Christian enterprise. He discussed rather objectively how the Penney Company projected its activities for the benefit of the business. At the time the corporate planners were working on first-quarter goals for 1981, nearly six years into the future.

It is likely that I was excited because the ideas and methods Seibert advocated so fully meshed with my own. But my excitement was quickly dampened by disappointment in the views of some of the men at the table where I sat. Some of their remarks included:

"I'm not sure that is biblical."

"Goals may work for a company, but not for a church."

"He may find that a good method, but goals aren't for everybody."

"If a person trusts the Lord he doesn't need goals."

"Setting goals seems to presume upon God."

I did not then, nor do I now, after several years of reflection, believe any of the five objections. They were sincerely offered, but that did not make them true or valid. The opposite of each objection affirms my own view. Biblical concepts of faith do encourage goal-setting. Goals do work well, as well as for churches as they do for corporations. They are for everybody—children, parents, professionals, laborers—anybody. Trusting God can be done at least as well, and I believe better, in a goal-oriented atmosphere.

Goal orientation is faith-oriented, expectant, and asks God to close doors if presumption is a problem. Which must be easier for God—to open doors or close them? He is quite competent to do either, but His will to prevent activity is as much to be advocated as His will to initiate it. This open/close perception was discussed in an earlier chapter. Goal orientation appears to take into favorable consideration a greater number of biblical principles than no goal orientation.

CREATING DEMANDS

The creation of dilemmas makes goal-setting appear difficult and confusing. Yet goals will, when effectively processed, dissolve dilemmas. The experience of one couple clarifies this point.

The young wife was not fully happy with her situation. Some of her friends were prospering by having both husband and wife work. She observed that they bought homes, automobiles and attractive clothes. But she and her husband were eking out an existence. She shared her periodic complaints with me and we talked at length about goals and priorities.

She and her husband had selected two magnificent goals which were delayed or lost to her friends. Getting a university education through a doctoral program was a primary goal for the husband. Having their children during their first years of marriage was also a goal. Both goals—education and children—

were worthy goals and preferred, in my opinion, above the first goals of their friends.

But judgment of the priority goals of any couple is not my concern, nor the concern of any other counselor. A counselor's concern is to point out that if a couple tries to gain affluence, property, an education, and have children they will likely encounter competing goals. To unrealistically cling to competing goals will create frustration, and may cause disillusionment with the goal-setting process. This couple had to learn that long-range goals for the development of their financial security made their current financial limitations tolerable.

Objectives do much for us. They reveal light at the end of the tunnel, but they are not miracles offering everything at once.

What you ought to say is, "If the Lord wants us to, we shall live and do this or that." Otherwise you will be bragging about your own plans, and such self-confidence never pleases God. Remember, too, that knowing what is right to do and then not doing it is sin (James 4:15-17).

CHAPTER SEVEN

Setting Goals—The Right Way

Goals may be satisfactorily set by following effective processes. These I have tried to identify and illustrate:

PREPARING IN ADVANCE

The goal-setter must be futuristic in his thinking. He must believe that what he wishes to happen in the future is important to its happening. His belief is primary to setting in motion the events that will cause his hope to come to pass. He cannot be positive he will succeed, but without a goal he is likely going to miss, as a marksman will likely miss a target unless he aims for it. Aiming for it, he may miss the center, but at least he hits somewhere on the target. If he tries for nothing he will get it—nothing.

During a conference in 1973 a gentleman

challenged my assertion that everyone should have goals. He stated that he did not need them, that he had a good job, nearly owned his home, drove a fine car, had a bank account and enjoyed a happy family. All members of the family were Christians, healthy and happy. His friendly protests did not persuade me. "All right," he said, "show me where I can make some goals."

"Go to the future," I replied. "I argued in my message this morning for the future. There is something in your future that can be achieved better with goals than without."

"Give me just one," he joked.

"Do you have any future house repairs? What kind of roof is on your house?"

"Asphalt shingles."

"How long have they been there?"

"About fifteen years."

"When must they be replaced?"

"About five years—1978."

"How will you pay for the roof?"

"With a home improvement loan."

"Why not set a goal for five years, figure costs, save the money and pay for it without a loan in 1978? Save a fifth of the cost each year and pay the bill at any time. By this means you will not have to pay any interest, and there is something special about the game of planning. Actually, the cost is reduced by the interest saved in paying cash and the interest on the savings for the project. This goal, if completed, will cost about twenty to twenty-five percent less than the way you plan to do things."

He acknowledged the benefit, and seemed surprised at his own acquiescence to my proposal. I do not know if he followed up on the idea, but he admitted at the time that he should. There were other advantages to advanced planning for him which included shopping for the best price with cash, considering alternatives like selling his home at an opportune time to upgrade his property holdings, and protecting himself against inflation. If he underestimated his costs and was forced to borrow, he would incur a lower debt in 1978.

SEEKING INFORMATION

Anyone planning his future, a future which is unknown, needs all the valid information he can gain. He may begin his search by talking out his interests with persons who know something about the areas or subjects relevant to decision-making in his field. If I believe that I should make career decisions, I should talk to persons with my interests. If teaching is the field, I should talk to teachers, especially representatives in the academic areas of interest to me. If law, I should talk to lawyers. If ministry, to ministers. If medicine, to doctors. If manual labor, to laborers.

The questions should be well designed before the interviews and an agreement on the amount of time to be occupied for the discussion should be determined in advance. Some will refuse to talk, or, if talking, will not be helpful. But there are always important persons who are supportive of anyone interested in their work. Even if rebuffed, the inquirer never gives up. He must be informed about the profession which may occupy his life.

Generally, inquirers must be dragged into reality. Few teachers are permitted to devote all their time to teaching. There are many onerous chores.

Attorneys write wills and letters, or make phone calls, or conclude a question about income taxes. And if they have a potential case for litigation there is only about a three percent chance it will make a court docket. The rest are settled out of court with compromise. The dramatic courtroom scenes in which a clever attorney saves his client from a lifetime prison sentence seldom appear in real life.

And minsters do not preach to thousand-member congregations as a rule. In the United States over half of church congregations number less than one hundred persons. The minister may expect to be paid a modest salary, will call upon parishioners with personal problems, study the Bible and other books, and work at meeting the expectations of men and women who are sometimes difficult to please. But the privilege of ministry is worth the personal sacrifice made.

Career inquirers should know the full story. They must be realistic about their lives and the future. Starry-eyed men and women with naive, stereotyped fantasies are forced to realism when they investigate real-life situations. Wrong ideas subside. On occasion disappointment sets in, but truth is ultimately appreciated. The purposes of service, commitment to values, and the like, emerge so that dreams are forced into practical considerations. When decisions are made on valid information, a person will ultimately feel more gratified with what he decides to do.

LISTING PROS AND CONS

The inquirer should list the advantages and disadvantages inherent in his proposed course of action. What is favorable? What is unfavorable? What barriers will he confront?

Is it possible for him to scale those barriers, or go around them, or even disregard them? Who will have to make sacrifices to assist him in his purpose? Will that person reap commensurate benefits sometime in the future, within a reasonable time frame? Numerous other questions require answers, such as: What are the educational requirements? What are the available opportunities? What circumstances pertain?

Once lists of benefits and problems have been completed and analyzed, a decision must be faced on whether or not the individual is willing to pay the price of achievement. Is the cost worth the results to be gained? The decision presumes that perceptions, talents, information, opportunities are clear to the decision-maker.

Achieving a large objective is costly in various ways, especially in taxing the spiritual/mental/emotional capacities of the persons involved. A goal, ideal on paper or in argument, may be totally unsatisfactory because the participants would pay too high a price for its attainment. They do not have the heart for it, or the risk appears to threaten other aims in their lives.

ADOPTING DEMOCRATIC PRINCIPLES

The person making a decision about some

project should be sensitively aware that his decision relates to the future experiences of others. If he has a family, his wife and children should have something to say about proposed events that will, if they do come to pass, affect their lives. Consensus should become an issue when more than one person is affected by a decision.

Although consensus is sometimes criticized as a weak or evasive way of making decisions, it is quite the opposite. Those nearest to us and most affected by our decisions likely also have insights which are important to analysis. They will help us avoid mistakes.

When my wife and I were considering moving from one career to another, from one city to another, we were careful to review all matters with our one remaining dependent child. Her views were important and guided us in the choices of several situations, including the high school she would attend. In fact, we shared our objectives with our adult children living away from us, to gain their opinions. They communicated their views, but concluded that it was our decision to make. Nevertheless, our longtime perception of family participation continued in the exchange, and the impression was good.

Seldom is goal-setting a solo effort. When others have afforded insights, they are more sympathetic with the effort and are more likely to contribute energy and resources to it. A person bent upon his own purposes runs the risk of exploiting others. He violates Christian principles if he utilizes anyone with that person's considered agreement, even a member of his own family.

Part of goal-setting which involves others is advocacy. Persuasion is part of the process. The goal-oriented person may have to delay his objectives until he has persuaded those who must accompany him in his venture. A goal is not, as some would have it, so generally overpowering that it is to be followed at any cost. Goals, as stated earlier, may be amended, dropped, and even reversed. Situations and persons change. Their goals change with them. To be forced to argue for one's goals, pleasantly but with enthusiasm, serves to maintain a check, a means of evaluating a goal, or several goals related to one another.

If feasible, an individual should make a trial run of an objective. He may be able to prove in a test situation that his concepts hold up in practice. Because he is dealing with some unknowns, as the future of anyone must be unknown, he should be wary of becoming presumptuous about his decisions. A trial run will, if nothing else, provide amendments to the original goal. For many, an interesting fallout from a test is an added sense of confidence. Not only did the goal look good on the planning sheet, it worked well in a laboratory situation.

The trial run is well demonstrated in numerous youth programs of recent years. For example, several church bodies have developed summer programs in camping, inner-city projects and missionary appointments. Young men and women in college are afforded opportunity during the summer to participate actively in meaningful experiences which relate to what they believe they might wish to do for a life's career.

If a collegian chooses to go abroad, is approved and accepted, he attends a seminar conference preparatory to travel. Arriving on the field, he is exposed to various opportunities and responsibilities during several weeks of intensive work and study. On occasion an appointee may remain for a year before returning to his homeland to complete formal education.

Churches and mission societies have discovered that a high percentage of their new permanent personnel have had experience in summer projects at home or abroad. It appears also that these persons make fine professionals. Their motivations were sifted out early in their search for a life's career.

After many years of working at my own career, teaching in a church-related college, I succumbed to an inner feeling and the arguments of several friends that I ought to teach in a public institution. But to be sure of the idea I accepted a one-year, part-time appointment at a state university while on a sabbatical leave from the college I served. I was completing a doctoral program, so I combined my interests for the year in order to analyze and test several objectives.

At the end of the year, although a fine full-time position in a university was available, I knew that my first purpose, to teach in a Christian college, would be the most gratifying for me. I felt deeply that I wished to teach students who, in their professional lives, would carry out similar ideals to my own. I returned to my former place.

PRAYING FOR GOD'S WILL

It is important to pray about goals for several reasons: to seek and find God's will, to moderate and energize ideas, to provide spiritual attitudes and insights, and to complete the biblical injunction relative to planning. This last is taught in Proverbs 16:1 and 9, used to conclude an earlier chapter: "We can make our plans, but the final outcome is in God's hands. . . . We should make plans, counting on God to direct us" (LB). And, from the New Testament: "What you ought to say is, 'If the Lord wants us to, we shall live and do this or that' " (James 4:15, LB).

Prayer reduces pride and can help us to develop improved thinking patterns. If a person applies standard processes, prayer is likely going to make him think through issues and act in less hasty ways than might otherwise be the case. Prayer invites larger insights than totally humanistic processes permit. Those insights and other prayer benefits cannot be easily analyzed. They are not subject to methodical explanation, but they are vital to Christian experience in all its departments, including objectives.

A man of my acquaintance worked for a wage of $13.00 an hour. He was offered a different position in another company for $7.50 an hour. His friends thought there was no question—take the higher salary. There is no way that I could decide to change jobs on so little evidence. Salary considerations are only part of the larger picture. Many Christian workers have chosen missionary careers and wages. Nearly all of them could greatly increase their incomes by taking other positions, even in Christian ministries. But they believe that if God's will in their lives means lower salaries, so be it. Worth is not measured in dollars. (It is to be deplored that even Christians may perceive their worth by the size of their paychecks.)

If missionaries rightly reject salary as a major motivation, why should not other Christians assume the same attitude? The man on the three-dollar-an-hour job may be, in his old job, more useful to society, more free for spiritual ministries, more at ease in his emotions, and the like. He should go through the process for decision-making in analyzing the new job offer, and he certainly should pray about the best course of action to be taken. Many factors play a part.

KNOWING HELP IS ON THE WAY

When the processes have been followed, and all is in order, the person may launch or pull back on his original goal. Assuming here that he is convinced of his objective, he begins doing the things that must be done to achieve success. He devotes time, resources, energy and self-sacrifice to the venture. He should be tenacious. The effort should not be diluted because emotions flag, or setbacks occur, or some other barrier interferes.

It is almost a truism that if one has a worthwhile goal, and is himself unable to do everything necessary to gain that objective, someone will come along to assist him on his way. This has occurred so many times in my own experiences and in the experiences of others I have observed that I have become convinced of a general axiom: If one is engaged in a meaningful effort to gain a worthwhile goal, someone will assist him to achieve it.

Illustrations of this general principle are common in my observation and experience. One man, needing more than a half million dollars for a worthy project, was aided by about thirty persons who volunteered assistance. A friend, with a large family, was able to finance a complete education through a doctoral degree. He was helped by about forty men and women who believed in him and what he determined to do. Other case histories are similar, and in the most dramatic situations the recipients seldom solicited the aid they received. (This is not to say that asking for help is objectionable.) Many persons wisely seek support for worthwhile ventures. Missionaries often are required to ask for support for their ministries.

My own experience has been as dramatic as any other I know. Following our marriage,

I determined to complete a college degree for the Bachelor of Arts. I had virtually no funds with which to support my small family. I took an early-morning job and a second job in the evenings. My mother, convinced I was going to maintain the educational goal, offered weekly assistance as I promised her I would lighten my work load. She was my goal saver during my senior year.

In 1957, I, with my wife and children, set a goal for me to earn a doctoral degree within ten years. My wife shifted her own life pattern and took a job which, at the outset, she knew she would resign from in ten years—even if the degree was not completed. The children agreed to duties and attitudes which would make it possible for me to work and study more than a family of four children would ordinarily permit. (This turned out to be a blessing in disguise, with the children focusing attention not on themselves but on a corporate set of goals. They matured more rapidly than otherwise would have been the case.)

Nearly three years slipped by, and although I was progressing, the rate of progress was not rapid enough to achieve the ultimate goal within the time frame we had set. We were somewhat disappointed, but we cast about for a means to catch up, even speed up, our schedule.

Another personal goal had been set to complete a book for a publisher in 1960. It was ready for the press, but the title was a matter of friendly debate between the editor and me. Because the president of the company was on another errand in my part of the country, he took on the duty of sifting out possible titles with me. We met in my home. While we were in discussion, I was called to my office, which was located about a half mile away from my home. Delayed for about an hour, I returned to discover my friend playing with our four children. The eldest was about fifteen and the youngest five years of age.

"Why don't you do what your children say you want to do?" he said.

"What have they been telling you?" I laughed at his gracious treatment of the children, and wondered what they had said.

"Each of them, when I asked about what they wanted to do with their lives, said they wanted to do what Dad wanted."

"What did they say?"

"I asked Jody, David, Mark and Sharon—one at a time—what was their prime goal in life. Each said he or she wished to help Dad get a doctorate. Children who support you like that should be encouragement enough for you."

"Yes, but they have a habit of eating,

wearing out clothes, and they need a roof over their heads. We have the goal, but it hasn't come together as yet."

"How much do you need to do it?"

"Maybe $5,000 more." (I greatly underestimated the cost.)

"You have it. My wife and I will see you through."

And they did. During the next few years they supported me in the completion of the program and in doing so invested $15,000 to pay my expenses. I do not see how the goal could have been successfully completed without their assistance. In addition, the publisher encouraged me in other professional opportunities in both writing and speaking. No protege could ever be treated more graciously than I was treated by this benefactor and his wife. But their involvement likely would have been limited if I had not presented a goal which they could identify with and support as part of their own ideals.

Several years after completing that doctoral program I was invited to become the president of a college. During the first months I learned the requirements of the job, and began to formulate goals for the institution. The college was constantly on the edge of financial failure. Although the operating budget income improved, there was barely enough to pay the bills. Nothing was available for capital improvements, even though the property was badly in need of renovation. Without improvement the college would not be able to hold students. The facilities were unsatisfactory and inadequate.

A friend, a member of the college board of trustees, discussed my concerns with his employer, who was a casual acquaintance of mine. The employer asked several questions about the college and me. He asked specifically about goals. He then suggested that I meet with him.

When my friend communicated the conversational exchange to me, I immediately arranged to fly to his city and meet with him. He was gracious, took me to lunch, and asked many questions, most of which related to the goals of the college. The goals had not been refined, and both of us knew it. I returned to San Francisco without special encouragement.

After a few months had passed I was invited to return for another meeting. The conversation was more encouraging, but no commitments were made. Again, I returned home empty-handed.

A few weeks later the gentleman came to

see me and the college. He urged me to continue to refine the goals. They were becoming more specific and were cast in clearer fashion. He promised a response, and left.

Meeting with his brothers, as trustees of a foundation, my new friend presented our case. They responded, and during the ensuing months accounted for $245,000 in capital funding, which broke the stalemate of the college on renovation. During four summers, stimulated by the support of that near quarter million dollars, the college renovated most of its property.

On one occasion I said to our benefactor, "You knew about the college for many years, your parents assisted it during the depression—why did you not help before this? And why did you aid us so generously now?"

"Simple," he said, matter-of-factly. "This is the first time any of us have seen any goals for your college." He would not recommend any institution, he said, that did not know where it was going. And direction had to be cast in goals.

It may be that the highest achievements have always been related to specific objectives made by the movers of the earth. Perhaps the idea of goal orientation is more ancient than we have imagined.

We have noted earlier in this writing that several Old Testament stories are clearly related to goal-setting. Solomon's experiences might make the most eminent example, especially his planning for temple construction and kingdom development. But a poignant story is also told in the first two chapters of Nehemiah, a story that illustrates the principle that a worthy goal of one person will be adopted by others to aid its achievement.

Nehemiah was convinced that the wall of Jerusalem should be built. He discovered that othing was being done—"the wall of Jerusalem . . . is broken down, and the gates thereof are burned with fire . . . when I heard these words . . . I sat down and wept, and mourned certain days, and fasted and prayed." Nehemiah included in his prayer a plea to God that the king would be sympathetic to his concern.

As Nehemiah, the cupbearer, served the king, his countenance was drawn because of distress for his beloved city. The king inquired about Nehemiah's appearance. Reluctantly, the cupbearer revealed himself, asking the king for temporary release so that he could go to Jerusalem to advance reconstruction. The king asked several questions, and responded to Nehemiah's requests, providing letters by which Nehemiah could requisition materials,

buoy the flagging spirits of the uncertain re-
turnees, and advance the project.

And he did it. He could not have achieved
it alone. He appears to have followed the right
processes: avoiding mistakes, making prepa-
rations, seeking information, praying for
God's will, and gaining support for his purpose. He may not have followed all the
steps—the narrative is silent about several—
but his attitude was fully that of a goal-setter.

*For which of you, intending to build a tower,
sitteth not down first, and counteth the cost,
whether he have sufficient to finish it? Lest hap-
ly, after he hath laid the foundation, and is not
able to finish it, all that behold it begin to mock
him, saying, This man began to build, and was
not able to finish (Luke 14:28-30).*

CHAPTER EIGHT

Achieving Personal Goals

I now wish to consider goals under two major divisions: personal and professional. In so doing, however, I do not mean to suggest that there are different standards for personal and professional interests.

In actual fact, there is an overlap. Each decision or goal affects every other decision. For example, my decision related to my work (professional) will certainly affect my wife (personal). This complexity is part of what makes goal-setting hard work.

The goal-setter is advised again: goals are specific and measurable; purposes are general and cannot be measured. Purposes may only be achieved as goals are set, followed and accomplished. The test of a goal is related to: 1) a practical time limit for its completion, and 2) a way in which an evaluator can determine whether or not the goal has been completed.

With these thoughts in mind, the following are some examples of worthy personal goals:

Spiritual. I may determine to read the Bible through in two years, to pray privately fifteen minutes each day, to maintain a monthly contact with a spiritually needy family, to read a leading Christian magazine once a week, to attend church twice weekly, to set aside a weekly period for reviewing my own spiritual growth and that of members of my family, and to tithe a tenth of my income as that income is earned.

(Each of the above is related to the purpose of spiritual growth in the person, and also in his family. Each can be verified by a family member and each is controlled in a time frame—two years, fifteen minutes daily, once-a-month minimum, weekly minimum, twice weekly, a weekly period.)

Physical. I may decide to exercise vigorously fifteen minutes each day in the morning and a half hour on non-working days except Sunday, to get an annual physical examination, to eat according to a specified diet which fits a physician's recommendation for daily intake, to give up a debilitating habit this year by incorporating a substitute to distract me.

(These may be supported by purposes and examined on the same criteria as other goals.

The criteria are implied in the statements of objectives for spiritual life development above—time frames and measurable characteristics.)

Educational. I may determine to earn a college degree in five years, to read a leading book once a month, to engage in at least one sophisticated conversation each week, to watch four educational television programs a month, to avoid any television of any kind for at least one day a week, to have one day a week when spare time is used for reading.

Geographic. I may decide to travel around the world during the next five years or before marriage and settling down, to live in the state of California, to purchase property where I might like to retire.

I trust an illustration related to geographic goals may be permitted here to show how a family may set and achieve a goal, amend it, and dissolve it, but find in their shifts what they were seeking.

After speaking at a conference center I was approached by one of the couples ecstatic about goal-setting. The man did most of the talking to me: my wife and his followed their own conversation.

"We have always wanted to live in Santa Barbara," he said.

"Why not move there?"

"Because my job is in Sacramento, and I have responsibilities. But my goal, for ten years, has been to move to Santa Barbara. What would you do?"

"I would move to Santa Barbara."

"Aw—come on! You can't just do that."

"I think you can, but it can be done in an orderly way."

"How?"

"Well, there are several ways. I would start by talking to my boss to discover if there will be an opening in Santa Barbara."

"Do you think that will work?"

"Probably not, but then we can go on to plan two."

"What is plan two?"

"Don't know yet, but there is one. Let's try the first and go from there."

He did try—and succeeded. A week after our talk I received a long distance telephone call from my friend: "We are going to Santa Barbara. I did what you said. The boss told me the company was opening a new office in Santa Barbara in about two years, and I can have a great position there. In the meantime, I am to move to Monterey for a year or so until Santa Barbara opens."

"Monterey! That's suffering, isn't it?"

"We are happy. I'll keep you posted."

Months went by. A call came in from my friend, "We want to go back to Sacramento. We discovered our friends, our church, our roots are there. We are homesick. How do we get back?"

"The same manner in which you got away. Talk to your boss again."

It worked, and the family returned to Sacramento. But the city and circumstances were different. There was no yearning for other pastures. Although they were back, attitudes, feelings, even energies, were changed for good, for the family's happiness. The move away and back were worth the effort.

A similar experience occurred to my wife and me. We decided, after our fiftieth birthdays, that we would like for our ultimate retirement to purchase a lot in a location we both loved. But lots were scarce for building. The few there were had been purchased and were firmly held by their owners. We decided on one that seemed to be just what we wanted.

I inquired about ownership and discovered it was owned by a man I knew, and with whom I served on the board of an institution. I was told by mutual friends that he would never sell. But my goal was set to purchase the lot. The friends laughed at my announcement.

The next time I saw the owner of the lot, I proposed purchase.

"My wife and I have owned that lot for over ten years. We will build on it someday. It isn't for sale," he said.

"Well, Bob, don't forget I'm a Christian and your business will go to pot if you don't sell that lot to me."

We both laughed. From time to time I nagged him about the lot, but without success. One day during spring, 1975, he phoned.

"You want that lot—you can have it." He named his price, turned the matter over to his lawyer, and left on a business trip to Paris. When he returned, the transfer was completed. My wife and I were thrilled, and walked over the land, speculating about our plans. Persons could not believe that the owner would sell. They offered more than we paid, but we refused, telling them that if they had set goals for it they would have purchased the property before us.

By 1977 the rise in taxes, the cost of maintenance, the pressure of building restrictions, the realization that our lives had become crowded with professional activities, all added up to a realization that we would not be able to build and use our "dream home." The goal of building would have to be drastically amended or dropped.

A man needed the lot. His work and purposes as a person in Christian ministries required him to locate in the vicinity. He contacted us by letter, making an offer which we accepted. We had decided *not* to put the property up for sale, but to sell if someone offered to buy and had family purposes which would be similar to our own.

The sale turned out to be beneficial to that young family. My wife and I not only profited financially from the short-term investment, but relaxed in ourselves relative to purchasing and holding property we cannot use for many years. Our purposes for retirement have been amended by our short landholding experience. Our present beliefs and animation about our lives would have been rewards enough to have purchased the lot and sold it at a loss. We are pleased that we risked something. As is usually the case, we profited in several ways.

But, we must return to our main line of thought—descriptions of personal goals.

Family. I may fix the time of marriage either following college or by my twenty-fifth birthday, to choose a wife whose interests are similar to my own, to have two children within the first five years of marriage, to live close to (or some distance from) our paternal parents.

Social. I may wish to join a service club as soon as I begin my first job, to date my wife once a week, to meet with friends on a periodic schedule, to make at least one new friend annually whom we would get to know in a meaningful relationship, to relate to the men and women of a church by attending the functions of the church as scheduled.

Material. I may determine to save at least a tenth of my income as that income is earned, to join an investment club which will meet at least four times yearly, to earn a specific amount of money annually, to build a house in seven years, to buy $100,000 insurance within three years.

The above personal goals may be added to, amended, or dropped—as suggested earlier in this writing. They require regular review and monitoring. They should be related to purposes which, among others, include the desire to become spiritually mature, to be physically healthy, to develop my mind to its greatest potential, to live in a climate which is attractive to my family, to establish and develop a happy family, to relate to other human beings with lasting friendships, to build an appropriate security for life and family and to support ideals in which I believe.

Remember . . . personal goals have personal profit!

These words spake Jesus . . . I have finished the work which thou gavest me to do . . . As thou hast sent me into the world, even so have I also sent them into the world . . . Neither pray I for these alone, but for them also which shall believe on me through their word . . ." (John 17).

CHAPTER NINE

Achieving Professional Goals

This chapter will focus attention on professional goals. Again, I have delineated and illustrated these under several categories:

My work. My purposes in life were gradually developed. The first serious aim was to become a minister. Within a few years after marriage I also determined to become a teacher without giving up my original purpose. Several years later I decided I wanted to write. At age forty-six I was invited to take an administrative post in a college and did so. At that point it became my purpose to develop myself as an administrator.

These four purposes became my foci, my distant lights, guiding the course of my professional life. Each was to be added to the other without replacing or displacing any other. Each was to be effectively treated, as my talents would permit, and each was to contribute to the others.

This interweaving proved to be a gratifying means of developing my own individuality. That which I preached about, I wrote about. The places in which I chose to speak tended to advance the institution I administered. Combining purposes created an unexpected efficiency.

But colleagues were sometimes offended by them. Some felt that I should give all my time to the ministry, or to teaching, or to administration. My view has been that as long as I am wanted in any of the areas I will accept the privileges of variety.

Goals related to the above purposes included such activities as: 1) writing a little each day for the books I wished to complete, 2) earning appropriate academic degrees within specified time frames, 3) finding persons with similar purposes to join with me or help me in various ventures for specified time periods and orientation, 4) accepting opportunities for one-, three-, or five-year time periods to carry through programs, 5) building college courses within stipulated time frames, 6) relating to persons with adequate expertise in areas of my interest, 7) maintaining active files of materials related to the interests and work of my life. Scores of other specific objectives were stipulated and followed. Not all succeeded, but a sufficient number did succeed to gratify me, and bring to pass the events for which I had hoped and prayed.

My company. My purposes in identifying with employers were rather clear at the outset of each professional turn in my life. I knew that I wanted to work primarily for Christian institutions. These institutions were to be evangelical in their perception of Christianity and evangelistic in their motivations. This included all relationships—to publishers, to churches, to colleges, or to other groups. It was my general purpose to contribute to the advancement of the ideals to which I was committed, something I felt I could not do as fully in other contexts.

However, it was not only my purpose to relate to secular situations for the purpose of serving, but also to avoid developing in myself the provincialism which my primary interests might create.

The purposes related to professional contacts I would make included, among others, the following: 1) to select the denominations with which I would work, 2) to carry specific responsibilities and assignments from the institutions with which I would relate, 3) to volunteer service for the advancement of projects, 4) to learn the history of related institutions, 5) to show loyalty, and the like.

Certainly, the goals inferred above had to be made specific and cast within time limitations. For example, I demonstrated loyalty by giving specific amounts of money to projects, by assuming obligations in addition to my standard assignments, and by relating to programs that were not particularly important to me. It was my deliberate opinion that my purposes would be more effectively carried through if I scheduled myself beyond standard expectations. Volunteerism was my own evidence of loyalty, even to the institution that paid my salary.

My advancement. My purpose was to advance only as my superior would evaluate my abilities. Because I was perceived to be an aggressive type of person, I determined that I would never apply for a position. (More of this unusual attitude later.) I did wish to advance as far as as I could, although there were no time limitations related to advancement. My sincere feelings were that work worth doing is noble, and I refused to get bored with it. Many acquaintances complained about their jobs and put them down as degrading. That appeared to me to be an error in judgment about work and self-evaluation. Any work that serves human needs must be noble.

My goals related to advancement were not well formed or strong. In retrospect, I believe they could have been designed more completely and effectively even without any concern for personal advantage. Most of my goals related to advancement were constructed after the advancement came to me. On at least two occasions goals were formed after extensive questions were asked by potential employers about my qualifications and intentions. Their interest aroused mine, and stimulated my investigations. In both instances I later used the ideas formulated by the experiences.

My earnings. My purposes related to earning a sufficient income so that my family would be cared for, modestly, but not be so limited as to create ill feelings in them about the Christian ministry. I had heard many children of parents who were in church ministries complain about their circumstances and treatment. Pastors' children were heard to resist the church because of the shabby treatment, the level of penury their families suffered. I determined that my children would not be embittered by the feeling that they were not fairly treated by the people they identified with the church. Among my purposes was the determination that outsiders would not set the life-style my family would follow.

Goals to accomplish those purposes changed as our family needs changed. For example, during 1943-44, my first year in church ministries and first year of marriage, I requested a fifteen-dollar weekly income from the congregation I served. This was considerably lower than the average church member earned. The salary was small enough, but there were no children or debts to require more. My bride and I eked out our living without complaint. Our only purpose was survival that first year.

But in 1960-61 we set $1,000 a month as our required income in order to take care of our family and complete a doctoral program. The differential from a very small income to a relatively large one did not represent a change in attitude about sacrifice, but a difference related entirely to the larger goals we developed in the second instance. A new or enlarged goal will, as noted elsewhere, affect other goals. So the purpose to improve my education naturally affected my income. It would violate my sense of Christian stewardship and my beliefs about the Christian and materialism to desire an increased wage simply to have more money, or to feed the human desire for recognition and reward. To desire more and to maintain Christian integrity, I must ask the questions, "For what purpose?" The question can be answered best by evaluating, with biblical insights, the purposes and goals of my life.

Peter Zimmerman, president of a financial planning firm, stated that among high income persons:

—more than half have no wills,
—many have little idea of family worth on the death of the breadwinner,
—most have inadequate tax counsel,
—less than half plan financially for their children's education,
—many don't know their company benefits.

Goal-oriented men and women put their affairs in order. Financial planning is only one of the departments, and touches on virtually all others. Generally, when financial goals are not well developed the remainder are also neglected.

In an attempt to advance the institution I serve, and assist the faculty-staff of the college to formulate and follow through on appropriate objectives for their lives, I set up what have become known as "January Interviews." The personnel receive a questionnaire a month in advance, a form designed in my office to focus on any issues which might be of interest and concern to the community. (Note Appendix 2 for the 1976 and 1978 forms.)

The first January series was greeted with skepticism. Two persons asked if this was a clever means for terminating several jobs. I assured them there was no such prospect. My purpose was affirmed—to discover their personal objectives in life and conclude what the college might do to assist them in their achievement. And the college goals were discussed with suggestions reviewed on how the personnel might assist the college purposes.

One member of the faculty was persuaded of my interest in his personal and family objectives. I asked about his most important professional goal.

"For ten years," he said, "my wife and I have talked about taking time out for me to complete a doctoral program."

"Ten years! Why didn't you go for that degree?"

"We didn't feel we could afford it. But we talk about it a lot."

"Go and do it."

"Are you trying to fire me?"

"Of course not. I am serious. You ought to go after that degree. Your job will be here when you return."

"Are you serious?"

"Never more serious. Make an appointment to come back a week from today at the same hour and inform me concerning your progress."

My friend left the office impressing me with his mixed emotions. He seemed animated and perplexed. The appointment was made.

The following week he came in. "We have decided to do it," he said. "But we are nervous about the decision."

We talked for a short period about how the decision might be implemented, and another appointment was scheduled.

When he returned the third time, he held a note in his hand. In the intervening week various persons and groups had pledged support to him and his family. He reviewed the list in order and, smiling, underlined the total monthly income, sufficient to see the family through to the conclusion of the goal.

"What's that figure down in the corner?" I asked.

"That's my monthly salary here at the college," he said. "Note that I will get more as a graduate student than teaching for you."

We laughed together, and gave thanks for the goodness of God. He concluded his duties with the college at the close of the spring term.

The family moved across the country, and the man entered graduate school. In three years he earned the degree he had wanted for so long. Even though we maintained our friendship during his doctoral work, when he completed the program his services were sufficiently in demand by other institutions that we could not persuade him to return. He is committed to a fine position, teaching graduate students.

Such is the life guided by goals.

After these things were ended, Paul purposed in the spirit, when he had passed through Macedonia and Achaia, to go to Jerusalem, saying, After I have been there, I must also see Rome (Acts 19:21).

CHAPTER TEN

Why Does Goal-Setting Work?

Henry David Thoreau, friend of Emerson and a careful observer of early American life, stated:

> Did you ever hear of a man who had striven all his life faithfully and singly toward an object and in no measure obtained it? If a man constantly aspires, is he not elevated? Did ever a man try heroism, magnanimity, truth, sincerity, and find that there was no advantage in them—that it was a vain endeavor?

Thoreau, like most philosophers, often cast his views in general terms, in ideals, in abstractions. He believed that persons ought to be sufficiently creative to work out specific applications in their own lives. He did so for himself. And when he did, he wrote simply and practically about what he did and what happened to him.

For two years he took to the woods and wrote about his adventure in *Walden* (a title from the German language which means woods or forest). On one occasion during his retreat his attention was arrested by a rock which he had earlier brought from the brook into his cabin. Periodically, he used it for a doorstop, but that use, he felt, was insufficient to keep the stone. He returned it to the brookside and was pleased to have it restored to its proper place.

Thoreau sought meaning, balance and tranquillity. After a couple of years he returned to general society from his cabin and related to other human beings. To become a recluse in the woods was not his ultimate purpose. He had to find purpose, like the rock, in the place where he belonged. In that understanding he designed his life. Involvement, with all its tensions, is preferred over escape and seclusion.

It is our privilege, especailly the privilege of Christians, to design our lives. The insightful Christian will do this, in humility, recognizing the authority and blessing of God as necessary ingredients in human plans. He is not operating independently, but cooperatively with God.

Many Christians pray that their lives will

be useful and happy. In numerous life experiences neither adequate usefulness nor fair amounts of happiness are found. Is it faulty prayer? Are these unrealistic fantasies, hopes without cause? Is God unwilling, in the natural world, to grant fulfillment, or is that reserved for heaven and its privilege?

My own view is that life is meant to be fulfilling, exciting and useful for those who, in faith, are willing to make their lives "happen"—as the current slang idiom casts the idea. Men and women can make things "happen," including the upgrading of their lives. The concept has been discussed in the preceding chapters in this book. Our lives are yet to be lived. How shall we live them?

PROBLEM SOLVING

Personal problem solving has not, by media reports, been highly successful during recent years. Men, women and children are in a mass market for counselors. Counseling has become a major industry. Doctoral graduates in psychology and counseling fields are in demand. They are offered a wide selection of choices and locations for professional opportunities. Their calendars are full of troubled clients seeking solutions to knotty and complex problems. And counselors have not been as highly effective as they wish to be in meeting the needs of their counselees. This is not for want of desire for success, nor for want of trying. Many human problems are resistant of therapy.

Professionals are acknowledging failure. Many publications inside and outside the field of psychiatry and psychology are presenting articles on the matter. Especially is the Freudian method under fire. The attempt to solve problems by probing for and theorizing about their sources has not worked well.

After speaking several years ago to a secular meeting of psychologists and other professional counselors, I was approached by a member of the audience who opened conversation by saying, "Your views sound religious to me. Are you talking about counseling or the comforts of religion?" My response was immediate and energetic. I was happy that he detected, in a secular meeting, that I was fixing my views in a religious context. More correctly, it would be a biblical context.

My focus at the meeting was on the future as the best orientation for problem solving. Persons who could bury the unhappy past and become goal oriented for the future would more likely solve problems than those who were searching their past lives. The idea, although not new to psychologists, was not at the time widely or intensively used by them. And the idea came to me, not from secularists, but from the Apostle Paul, writing in Philippians, chapter three.

Early in the chapter the apostle referred to the "confidence of the flesh." He recited his own pedigree as an orthodox Jew, zealous in his support of the law. But these positive experiences and affirmations were insufficient to solve his personal problems. With all the effort for excellence he remained imperfect. Even so, he fully recognized that he was more mature at the time of the writing than during any previous period. He was advancing, which was exactly his purpose.

The Apostle Paul could also have recited his failures, in something of a self-purging, and added a follow-up "Freudian" analysis. He had been guilty of the worse sin—murder or consent to murder. He was prejudiced and self-righteous. But he rejected both the brave and the profane in his life before this very moment, and wrote instead: "Forgetting those things which are behind, and reaching forth unto those things which are before, I press toward the mark."

Paul, the Christian, discovered the truth of goal-setting (future orientation) as the effective means of problem solving in personal lives. It was not his method to trace a mental-emotional disturbance backwards to the treatment of a harsh parent, to the collapse of a nipple, to the death of a mate, to the rejection of a friend, to the loss of status. To him the only real thing would be the future. As noted earlier, even the present is an infinitesimal pinpoint dividing the past from the future.

The past can be instructive, but in the matter of personal problem solving, confession of past failures, acceptance of God's forgiveness and self-forgiveness, and appropriately putting the past out of mind ("forgetting those things behind") are prelude to the forward look. Errors of the past virtually erase themselves when an individual designs a future which rehabilitates, energizes, achieves, and directs something within him.

Purposes and goals are access lines to the future, to problem solving. The past is a matter of record, the future must wait for the record of itself, a record which individuals have some say in producing.

FUTURISM AND ROLE MODELING

Futurism, since the decade of the 1960s, has become an important field of study at several higher educational institutions. The better business colleges and departments are affirming the vital activity of analyzing and planning for the future. In one of his syndicated columns, widely circulated, on futurism, Arthur R. Roalman of Chicago introduced his article, "Why Corporations Hate the Future," with a quotation from an eminent president of a leading auditing firm:

> "Maybe 95 percent of all companies don't pay attention to the future," says Dale H. Marco . . . "They react to history—history that is anywhere from one day to a few centuries old . . . About 4½ percent of companies try to guess what's ahead. But they do it in such haphazard fashion that they guess wrong as often as they guess right . . . That leaves about ½ of 1 percent of the nation's companies that work hard and well at projecting the future. They know that today you can see the long-range impact of emerging technologies. These companies are right much more often than they are wrong. They are highly profitable, have relatively few inefficiencies, are fun and exciting places to work, and are great places to enjoy a long, rich career."*

However, Roalman believed, in 1975, that there were signs of improvement for planning

---

MBA Communications, Inc., 1975.

in the establishment of organizations like The World Future Society, whose purpose is to study "alternative futures." Other groups and programs advertise interesting themes for seminars and publications to aid persons and corporations to perceive the future and act accordingly. One of the programs is the "Futures Weeks" sponsored by many high schools.

An Illinois mathematics teacher, Robert Mercier, was quoted by Roalman:

> Students have been growing apathetic in the face of awesome changes all of us have seen in recent years. Their attitude, increasingly, is one of resignation, of inability to cope. Futures Weeks are one way of showing them that change is inherent to society, how to recognize change, and how to cope with it.

To complete his case on the growth of futurism, Roalman stated that Julia Larson, librarian for the World Future Society Book Service, estimated that in 1966 there were two books on the subject. In 1975 there were 140. But with all the emphasis, stated Roalman, "Much current planning is little more than projecting into the future what has happened in the past."

The columnist rightly followed his initial

observations with the argument that long-range planning works only when there is a real commitment to it, especially on the part of managers who will put plans into effect, if they are to be in effect in business. But problems prevent effective planning, like the Persian messenger syndrome ("where the bearer of bad tidings is beheaded by the king"), or the Jeane Dixon syndrome ("planning as an effort to predict the future"), or the solution-to-everything syndrome ("planning as a sure-fire solution to everyday problems . . . when they discover it is not . . . abandon planning altogether").

Roalman's observations about business planning are analogous to the problems of individual or personal goal-setting—long and short range.

If the future were not important to the present state of the Christian, prophecy would not be so vital to the biblical account. The future is important to God, and only He knows it. He has had much to do with its formation. Because we should, as we are able on the natural level, follow the example of the creative gestures of God, the future becomes a point of active present interest to us.

Daniel, becoming aware of the prophetic

captivity, began earnest prayer that the promise would be fulfilled.

After presenting counsel to the Philippians about forgetting the past and turning energies to the future, the Apostle Paul suggested that following the example of persons like himself, future oriented, would aid those who needed to learn how to focus on the future.

Students of Pauline writings are well aware of the repetition of futuristic principles in the author's epistles. The apostle urged the Corinthians to run in a race "not stumbling." Stumbling is caused by looking backward while the body is propelled forward. Or the runner may look down or away and lose equilibrium. Pace is broken. The principle for effective running is to fix upon a goal ahead and strive for it. Those who win will have had their future goals in mind, and then in sight. In most instances they will achieve them.

Once an individual is able to perceive what goals are, he is not threatened by them. They are no longer matters of morality in their achievement or failure. Their magnitude sometimes creates awe, even trauma, but they may be conquered by efficient management which breaks them down into practical and controllable subgoals. When the subgoals (short range) are accomplished, the large ones (long range) are completed.

GOALS AND TIME PLANNING

Most writers about goals make time management a major issue in understanding what goals are and how they may be constructed. Alan Lakein was generally acknowledged to be the leading and most active professional in time management. Lakein related time and goals, pointed out Jane O'Reilly:

> It takes organization and concentration to carve out your own time, but most important of all it takes self-knowledge to *know what you want to do with it*. Without goals and motivation the time will evaporate. "A typical best use of time is to plan," says Lakein. Some people don't even make lists, much less imagine that today is connected with next week and five years from now. "But you can't effectively plan the next few days without deciding on the next ten years," says Lakein.*

To initiate his program, sorting out priorities, Lakein asked a series of questions and introduced processes for assuring results. The questions included:

1. What are your lifetime goals?

---

*Reader's Digest, July, 1972, p. 89.

2. How would you like to spend the next five years?

3. How would you like to live if you knew you would be dead six months from today?

These questions force the interviewee to work out contradictions, articulate interests, and settle on what is truly important to him.

Lakein tends to meld together time management and goal orientation. One is not meaningful without the other. O'Reilly quoted Lakein in relating the two concepts:

> "Most people don't think in terms of minutes," said Lakein. "They waste all their minutes. Nor do they think in terms of their whole life. They operate in the mid-range of hours or days. So they start over again every week, and spend another chunk unrelated to their lifetime goals. They are doing a random walk through life, moving without getting anywhere." *

GOALS AND WELL-BEING

Perhaps the most gratifying feature for goal-setters is the sense of well-being that goals afford. This comes in two ways. The first relates to excitement. To have a goal in mind and work for its accomplishment is an exciting venture. It tones the body, mind and

---

*Reader's Digest, July 1972, p. 79.

spirit. Goal-oriented persons seem healthier, happier and more confident than nongoal-oriented persons. They appear to be at the controls, to be leaders, and to be problem solvers. Nongoal-oriented persons seem to be troubled, rather than animated, with problems. They are more likely to blame others for failure or omission for which they should take responsibility.

The second advantage is the human sense of accomplishment. It is better to have a goal, work for it, and gain it than to find a windfall which is larger than the goal. It is better to earn a fortune than inherit it—if all activity is ethical. It is better to earn an academic degree than have one given. It is better to take responsibility to pay one's own bills than to have someone else pay them. It is better to build from the beginning than to step into something already well-ordered. This does not mean that established institutions are to be denigrated. The point is between that which is good and that which is better.

Goal-oriented persons plan. They plan their own development, their career, their family, their budget, their spiritual life, their retirement, and other matters. They are unwilling to leave life to chance.

Goal-setting works because it turns on

lights in the darkness. It works because it maps, no matter how clumsily, the future. It works because it has been proven by armies of persons who, having experimented with goals, affirm their effectiveness. It works because it calls upon all the qualities of a person to tax himself to his greater potential.

Perhaps it works because it is the pattern used by God, Who in His divine plan made the worlds and all that in them is. And when that plan confronted barriers, other goals were affirmed and activity set in motion. In this perspective Jesus Christ was prophetically placed, and, in line with the detailed objectives, entered the world through incarnation, lived, taught, worked, died and resurrected— according to plan. That plan, with its goals, is not yet completed. But it will be.

I would like to guide my life with similar purposeful patterns.

Brethren, I count not myself to have apprehended: but this one thing I do, forgetting those things which are behind, and reaching forth unto those things which are before, I press toward the mark . . . (Philippians 3:13-14a).

Read a Little More

John W. Alexander. MANAGING OUR WORK. InterVarsity Press, Downers Grove, Illinois. Second Revised Edition. 1975.

Richard Nelson Bolles. WHAT COLOR IS YOUR PARACHUTE? Revised. Ten Speed Press, Berkeley, CA. 1972.

Peter F. Drucker. THE EFFECTIVE EXECUTIVE. Harper and Row, New York. 1966, 1967.

Ted W. Engstrom and Edward R. Dayton. THE ART OF MANAGEMENT FOR CHRISTIAN LEADERS. Word Books, Waco, Texas. 1976.

Ted W. Engstrom and R. Alec MacKenzie. MANAGING YOUR TIME. Zondervan Publishing House, Grand Rapids, Michigan. 1967.

Charles Hummel. TYRANNY OF THE URGENT. InterVarsity Press, Downers Grove, Illinois.

James L. Johnson. THE NINE-TO-FIVE COMPLEX. Zondervan Publishing House, Grand Rapids, Michigan. 1972.

Appendix 1. Goal Outline— Planning

SIMPSON COLLEGE
San Francisco

OFFICE OF THE PRESIDENT

December 16, 1975

To: FACULTY/STAFF

Re: January Interviews

Each full-time employee should make an appointment with my office for an interview during the month. The staff people should precede the faculty members. I prefer to talk to faculty persons after their conversations with the Academic Dean.

Part-time employees are welcome to arrange an appointment, but it is not required.

Attached are copies of a questionnaire. Will

you give careful attention to the questions and
prepare for our talk together?

_____

President

MWL:yc
Attachment

Mark W. Lee   Simpson College
President   San Francisco

Goals

Philosophy _____
_____

I. PERSONAL—What would you like to make happen for yourself? _____
_____
_____

  A. Spiritual _____
_____

  B. Physical _____
_____

  C. Educational _____
_____

  D. Professional _____
_____

  E. Social _____
_____

  F. Family:
    1. Job _____
_____

    2. Savings _____
_____

    3. Home _____
_____

4. Recreation_____

_____

5. Retirement _____

_____

6. Other_____

_____

7. Other _____

_____

II. INSTITUTIONAL—What do you wish to
see in the institution you work for?
A. Company _____

_____

B. Administration _____

_____

1. Supervisory _____

_____

2. Staff _____

_____

3. Labor_____

_____

C. Departments _____

_____

_____

D. Profits _____

_____

_____

E. Size_____

_____

_____

F. Other _____

_____

G. Other _____

_____

CONCLUSIONS: What goals do for us.

Long Range _____

Short Range _____

Controls _____

_____

Communications _____

_____

Evaluations _____

_____

(ML/y/1/78)

Appendix 2. Evaluation—On the Job

SIMPSON COLLEGE

San Francisco

OFFICE OF THE PRESIDENT

January, 1976

To: FACULTY and STAFF

Re: January Interviews

The following questions may assist us in our conversations this month. If you find some of the queries unsuitable to your situation, pass over them. Do not wrestle with the meanings of the questions. On those which do apply, you should give some preparation so that we can extract the most good from the time we have together. Some of you may wish to prepare an introductory statement to initiate the conversation. I am eager to plan details to gain the greatest amount of feedback from you. *At the time of the interview* bring this questionnaire filled out for my use so that discussion will move along. I will use the copy on which you have penned responses.

Read through the document before answering any question. Two copies of the questionnaire are being sent to you. More may be secured from the President's Office.

1. Was your work performance evaluated during the last twelve months? _____ .
   If so, what were the significant factors?
   Affirmative: _____

   _____

   Needing improvement: _____

   _____

2. Would it be helpful to develop in-service programs to assist you in your work?____ .
   What type of program would you like to have inaugurated? (If you had a program, use this space to evaluate it; e.g., the Supervisor Seminar with the Business Manager.)

   _____

   _____

   _____

3. The college offers the following privileges to the faculty and staff. Do you take advantage of them?

	Never	Sometimes	Usually	Nearly Always
a. Noon meal	___	___	___	___
b. Faculty chapel	___	___	___	___
c. Staff chapel (once weekly)	___	___	___	___
d. Prayer meetings	___	___	___	___
e. Faculy/Staff socials	___	___	___	___
f. Trustee banquets	___	___	___	___
g. Morning coffee breaks	___	___	___	___
h. Afternoon coffee breaks	___	___	___	___

Should any of the above be eliminated? ___
If any, which ones? _____
_____

Should any be added? _____
_____

If any, what should they be?_____
_____

4. Assuming that you understand the immediate potential of the college resources, what do you believe ought to be the next projects of the college?

   a. For the students _____
   _____

   b. For the faculty_____
   _____

   c. For the staff _____
   _____

   d. For the institution as a whole _____
   _____

5. Rank the items in #4 (above) in the order of importance you attach to them, with

one (1) ranking highest, and four (4) ranking lowest:

a._____, b._____, c._____, d._____

Remarks: _____

6. What is your evaluation of the service performance and attitudes in the following
departments:

Superior Excellent Good Fair Poor

a. College Services
   (mailing, phones, etc.) ___ ___ ___ ___ ___
b. Food Service
   (dining hall) ___ ___ ___ ___ ___
c. Machine Shoppe
   (vending machines) ___ ___ ___ ___ ___
d. Business Office (courses,
   admissions, etc.) ___ ___ ___ ___ ___
e. Academic Offices
   (courses, admissions,
   etc.) ___ ___ ___ ___ ___
f. President's Office
   (communications,
   response, etc.) ___ ___ ___ ___ ___
g. Student Deans' Offices
   (counseling, dormitory,
   rules) ___ ___ ___ ___ ___
h. Janitorial Service
   (paper pickup,
   cleaning, etc.) ___ ___ ___ ___ ___
i. Maintenance Service
   (repairs, etc.) ___ ___ ___ ___ ___
j. Simpson College
   Foundation ___ ___ ___ ___ ___
k. Student Council (partici-
   pation, purpose, etc.) ___ ___ ___ ___ ___
l. Library
   (service, hours, etc.) ___ ___ ___ ___ ___

m. Book Bay (ordering
   texts, service, etc.)   ___ ___ ___ ___ ___
n. Faculty relations
   and rapport   ___ ___ ___ ___ ___
   Staff relations
   and rapport   ___ ___ ___ ___ ___
   Faculty/Staff relations
   and rapport   ___ ___ ___ ___ ___
o. Kaiser Medical
   (service, etc.)   ___ ___ ___ ___ ___

Remarks: _____
_____

7. What do you believe to be the three strong-
   est academic departments of the college?
   a. _____, b. _____,
   c. _____

What do you believe to be the three weakest
academic departments of the college?
   a. _____, b. _____,
   c. _____.

8. Are you achieving your personal ambitions
   in your work at Simpson College? Explain.
   _____
   _____
   _____

These forms are being reproduced on paper of
different colors so as to differentiate between
staff and faculty responses. It is assumed,
then, that each member will be aware that the
college will know to what issues and on what

bases the responses are made. The questions grow out of ideas expressed to me by various persons or groups at the college.

I must assume that if I have missed any points which you feel are vital to the ongoing of an effective college, you will introduce them. I very much appreciate your attention to the questionnaire. Your opinions are valued.

_____

President
MWL:yc

SIMPSON COLLEGE
San Francisco

OFFICE OF THE PRESIDENT

January, 1981

To: FACULTY and STAFF

Re: January Interviews

As you know, January is our date to discuss personal and institutional matters as they affect each of us. There is no set time limit for these conversations. Some are short (10 minutes or so), many are longer than half an hour. New faculty/staff personnel may wish to chat with older members so that they will be at ease. This is not supposed to be a threatening exercise.

To assist us in these talks, a questionnaire or worksheet has been provided each year. No two of them have been the same, although some questions reappear from time to time as we seek to measure progress. The annual interviews have contributed significantly to the progress of the college and the realization of some of the personal goals of our people. Two copies of this worksheet are provided. *Fill one out for me and give it to me at the time of the interviews.*

All full-time personnel should make appointments for interviews. Part-time persons are not required to make appointments, but may do so if they wish. Faculty members should arrange a meeting after their interview and evaluation session with the Academic Dean. Staff people should come in first—early in January.

Do not read "second or hidden meanings" into the questions. We will clarify differences of interpretation during the interview. I accent again—it is my hope that each person will give careful preparation to this questionnaire. Read the document in its entirety before answering any question.

You will discover in this approach that I am following up the papers and questions which were used and discussed during and after the Faculty Conference in late August. Anyone wishing to have a copy of my paper to the faculty at that time may receive one from my office.

1. Do you have any personal concerns which you would feel free to share with me? _____
   _____

   a. Family _____
   _____

   b. Goals _____
   _____

   c. Problems _____
   _____

   d. Future _____
   _____

2. How do you feel about any aspect of the following:
   a. Retirement: How it ought to be initiated? Carried through? Policies?
   _____
   _____
   _____

   b. Job description: Do you know what your job assignment entails? What is required? What you would like to see done?
   _____
   _____
   _____

c. Community: Do we have "community" at the college? What more may be done? Do we need it?

_____
_____
_____

d. Scholarship: Are we a scholarly faculty? What more may be done? Are you scholarly?

_____
_____
_____

e. Service: Are you aware of the service orientation of the college? Do you support it? What more may be done?

_____
_____
_____

f. Work load: Are you gratified with your work assignment? Should it be smaller? Larger? Is the load evenly distributed at the college?

_____
_____
_____

3. What about the moral and spiritual life of the college?
   a. What do you do to contribute to the spiritual life and integrity of the college?

_____

_____

_____

b. What is your relationship and attitude toward Chapel?

_____

_____

_____

c. What is your relationship and attitude toward announced prayer periods for faculty/staff?

_____

_____

_____

d. What is your opinion of the rules of the college?

_____

_____

_____

4. How may the administration of the college improve:
   a. Evaluation _____

_____

_____

   b. Communications _____

_____

_____

   c. Availability _____

_____

_____

d. Leadership _____

_____

_____

e. Spiritual life _____

_____

_____

f. Direction _____

_____

_____

5. What (if anything) may be done to:
   a. Gain support for special events (like Faculty Forum)

   _____

   _____

   _____

   b. Gain support for the college:
      1) In student recruitment _____

      _____

      2) In funds for capital improvements

      _____

6. Remarks: _____

_____

_____

_____

_____

The administration fully expects to advance salaries and wages for the 1978-79 school year. The increases are expected to be the largest the college has had during my tenure here. If they are to rise and continue to improve, there must be some improvement in productivity. Sometimes this is found in more efficient ways of doing work so that time may be freed for other things worth doing for the good of the order. We may talk generally about this matter and there will be reassignments, principally for some faculty members, to improve the performance of the whole college. Think in terms of suggesting improvements which may relate to adjustments in our roles. For example, the staff has been reduced by four members during the last year. Wages for staff will average at least a twelve-percent increase next year as a result. Do you believe the change in staff size has been beneficial? Could faculty changes also be made which would be profitable to the college and the faculty personnel? These and other questions you may wish to address.

DO CALL MY OFFICE AND MAKE AN APPOINTMENT.

_____

President

MWL:yc

(12/22/77)